IMAGES OF WAR

U-108 at War

IMAGES OF WAR
U-108 at War
RARE PHOTOGRAPHS FROM WARTIME ARCHIVES

ALISTAIR SMITH

Pen & Sword
MARITIME

First published in Great Britain in 2012 by
PEN & SWORD MARITIME
an imprint of
Pen & Sword Books Ltd,
47 Church Street,
Barnsley,
South Yorkshire.
S70 2AS

A CIP record for this book is available from the British Library.

ISBN 978 1 84884 667 8

Typeset by
Mac Style, Beverley, East Yorkshire

Printed and bound in England
By CPI Group (UK) Ltd, Croydon, CR0 4YY

Pen & Sword Books Ltd incorporates the Imprints of Pen & Sword Aviation,
Pen & Sword Family History, Pen & Sword Maritime, Pen & Sword Military,
Pen & Sword Discovery, Wharncliffe Local History, Wharncliffe True Crime,
Wharncliffe Transport, Pen & Sword Select, Pen & Sword Military Classics,
Leo Cooper, The Praetorian Press, Remember When,
Seaforth Publishing and Frontline Publishing

For a complete list of Pen & Sword titles please contact
Pen & Sword Books Limited
47 Church Street, Barnsley, South Yorkshire, S70 2AS, England
E-mail: enquiries@pen-and-sword.co.uk
Website: www.pen-and-sword.co.uk

Contents

Introduction

This unique album belonged to a member of the crew of the Type IXB U-108, which was then commanded by Kapitan-Leutnant Klaus Scholtz. The photographer and owner of the album, Willi Wilke, is thought to have been a member of the torpedo crew, with the rank of Obermechanikermaat.

What is particularly significant about this photographic album is the fact that it chronicles the events surrounding the U-108 between October 1940 and September 1942, whilst Wilke was a member of the crew. Of equal significance is the fact that at least four of the photographed members of the crew, who then held more junior officer posts, went on to command their own u-boats. These include Heinz Konrad Fenn, who would go on to command the U-139 and U-445, Paul Karl Loeser, who would command the U-30 and the U-373, Herbert Neckel, who would become commander of the U-531 and Otto Fechner, who would command the U-164.

The U-108 would have an illustrious career, undertaking some eleven active patrols from October 1940 until April 1944. The vessel would also be involved in seven major Wolfpack operations from June 1941 to April 1943. The U-108 is credited with the sinking of at least twenty five vessels, with a tonnage of nearly 119,000tons. She is also credited with the sinking of an auxiliary warship of over 16,000tons.

The U-108 was sunk after a bombing attack at Stettin in early April 1944. She was salvaged but never returned to active service. The u-boat was finally scuttled at Stettin on April 24 1945.

The original commander of the crew of twenty seven men, Klaus Scholtz, had been in the German navy since 1927. He would end the war as a Fregattenkapitan, having been awarded the Knight's Cross and the Knight's Cross with Oak Leaves.

Amongst the photographs in the album is a much debated incident, which in the album is noted as showing the sinking of the SS *Effna* on February 28 1941, just before midnight. However the photographs seem to suggest that an entirely different vessel may be actually featured, or that the official reports regarding the sinking of the vessel are incorrect. Instead of referring to the incident in February 1941 it has been suggested by several u-boat experts that the photographs illustrate two different incidents, both of which took place in June 1941, during the U-108's third active patrol. This patrol lasted for six weeks, seeing them sink seven vessels. If this is the case, then the photographs may well show the sinking of the Greek merchant ship, *Nicolas Pateras,* from Convoy OB366 on June 25 1941 and the Greek vessel *Dirphys* on June 8 1941.

The term u-boat is an Anglicised version of Unterseeboot, or U-Boot. U-boats had been successful during the First World War, but by the interwar years enormous advances had been made and the Germans, with a limited surface fleet as a result of restrictions imposed upon them by the Treaty of Versailles, had the largest submarine fleet. The u-boats were seen as a primary means by which the far superior Royal Navy could be defeated. Like many of the other u-boats that were operational during the Second World War, the U-108 would operate in the Atlantic and in the North Sea. They would take part in joint operations with other u-boats, known as Wolfpacks, to hunt and destroy whole convoys and their escorts. The heyday of the u-boat lasted until 1943; by then the Allies had developed sonar and radar and had broken German naval codes. This would lead to unprecedented losses in the German u-boat fleet. Ultimately the crippling of the u-boat threat would allow the Allies to launch amphibious landings in Africa, Italy and in Normandy.

Some eighty per cent of all German u-boats deployed during the Second World War would be lost to enemy action. They had managed to sink 14.5 million tons of Allied shipping. This was the equivalent of having sunk or destroyed 3,000 vessels. In exchange some 800 u-boats were lost.

This photographic album is owned by James Payne. The authors are indebted for his permission to use these photographs, as a record of not only one of the most famous and successful u-boats, but also of the legendary Klaus Scholtz.

Scholtz would survive the war. By the time France was well on its way to liberation in the late summer of 1944 he was based at Bordeaux, as commander of the 12th Flotilla. He had been in command of the unit since October 1942; just a month after Willi Wilke had left the vessel himself.

There is an incredible story of Scholtz's attempt to escape capture in August 1944. The bulk of the u-boats had left Bordeaux, bound for Flensburg and the 12th Flotilla was broken up. Scholtz led over 200 men in a bold attempt to escape across France to Germany. They set off on August 26 1944 but they were rounded up by American forces on September 11. Scholtz would spend some eighteen months as a prisoner of war. In the post-war period he served in the naval part of the Federal Frontier Guard (1953-1956) and then transferred to the German navy. Scholtz went on to become base commander in various locations, finally retiring with the rank of Kapitan zur See in 1966. He died at the age of seventy nine on May 1 1987.

As with many photographic albums relating to both the First and Second World Wars, it is impossible to tell what became of the owner of this album, Willi Wilke. The album contains a signed photograph of Scholtz, dedicated to Willi Wilke, however until recently Willi Wilke was not even listed as a member of the crew of the U-108.

Signed photograph of Klaus Scholtz dedicated to Willy (Willi) Wilke.

This portrait of Willi Wilke was taken shortly after the commissioning of the U-108 in 1940.

Chapter 1

Commissioning

The U-108 was a Type IXB u-boat, fourteen of which were commissioned and built between 1937 and 1940. The U-108 was one of the biggest batch of Type IXBs built in the period 1938 to 1940 and designated 971 and part of a series that would become U-103 to U-110. Like all of the other Type IXBs they were constructed at Ag Weser in Bremen. This shipyard had been involved in u-boat production since February 1936 and the last actual launch was the U-3051 on April 20 1945. In all some 162 u-boats were commissioned from this shipyard.

The Type IXB was an improved version of the Type IX. It had a range of around 1,500 nautical miles and its main offensive armament was twenty two torpedoes. The vast majority of the fourteen u-boats commissioned would sink at least 100,000tons of Allied shipping.

The U-108 was ordered in May 1938 and work began on her in late December 1939. She was launched in mid-July 1940 and the bulk of these photographs relate to the commissioning of the vessel on October 22 1940.

This photograph shows the officers of the U-108 during the commissioning ceremony. The vessel was built by Aktien-Gesellschaft Weser. It was a major German ship-building business, based on the Weser River at Bremen. The business had been established in the mid-nineteenth century and had been involved in the construction of u-boats during the First World War. This culminated in the launching of some ninety six vessels. Following a merger in 1926 the ship-building facilities at Bremen became one of the most important for Germany. The yard built around 150 u-boats during the Second World War. In 1939 around 16,000 people were employed at the shipyard, but towards the latter half of the Second World War a number of forced labourers and prisoners of war also worked there.

Kapitan-Leutnant Klaus Scholtz is seen here, on the conning tower of the U-108 during the commissioning ceremony. Scholtz had begun his naval career in 1927 and served on a number of torpedo boats. When this photograph was taken, in October 1940, he was a relative newcomer to the u-boat force. He had only joined it in the April. The captain and crew undertook four months of intensive training before the commissioning ceremony. Initially the U-108 was attached to the 2nd U-Boat Flotilla (October 1940 to August 1943).

Members of the crew of the U-108 are standing to attention on the deck of the u-boat during the commissioning ceremony. A Type IX u-boat would have around a fifty man crew. The organisation revolved around a number of officers, chief petty officers, petty officers and seamen. Amongst the officers and the seamen were a number of technical posts. Wilke was one of those seamen that had specialist skills, in this case related to the torpedoes. The command of the vessel usually comprised of four officers. It is fortunate in this album that the specific officers are not only named but their ranks are also clearly given. Scholtz would, of course, have held ultimate responsibility. His second in command, known as a First Watch Officer, or 1WO, would effectively take command if something happened to the captain. He would also be responsible for the weapon systems and torpedoes. The Second Watch Officer (2WO) was responsible for the flak gun and deck gun, the radio room and the watch crew on deck. The fourth and equally important officer was the Leading Engineer. Essentially he was an experienced mechanic and his other unwelcome duty was ensuring that the demolition charges were set properly should the u-boat need to be scuttled. This meant that in cases like this large numbers of Leading Engineers were lost as they went down with the vessel.

A senior Kriegsmarine officer is carrying out an inspection onboard the U-108 during the ceremony. On close inspection this senior officer appears to be Vize Admiral Karl Donitz, who was an experienced u-boat captain during the First World War. He became the commander of the German u-boat fleets in 1936. One of his sons, Peter, was killed onboard the U-954 on May 19 1943, when the boat was sunk with all hands in the North Atlantic.

This photograph pinpoints precisely where the U-108 was built and commissioned in Bremen. Deutsche Schiff und Maschinenbau AG, or Deschimag, was one of a number of shipyards that were merged with AG Weser. The company had been founded in 1926 and by 1941 it was largely owned by Krupp.

This photograph shows the captain and crew of the U-108 in December 1940. The photograph was taken two months after the commissioning ceremony and by this time the u-boat had transferred to its operations port of Wilhelmshaven. It was still six weeks or more before the U-108 would leave on its first operational mission. After June 1940 part of the 2nd U-Boat Flotilla, of which the U-108 was a part, would be based in Lorient in France. By June 1941, in order to aid operations in the Atlantic, the flotilla would be exclusively based in Lorient.

This second photograph, taken in December 1940, shows the crew wearing the short, waist-length jacket, or monkey jacket, which was often used for parades. Normally they would prefer to wear their denim working jackets, either in olive or green/brown colour, which would be more practical than their white clothing. The men are wearing a dark blue, woollen side cap. There had been an enormous expansion of the u-boat fleet in the period 1939–1943. Initially enough men graduated from the training schools each year to crew around sixteen submarines, but by 1940 this was increased to fifty four, 250 by 1941 and 350 by 1942.

Officers and crew are standing on the deck of the U-108 here, alongside a larger surface vessel. In the early stages of the war a u-boat commander had to be at least twenty five years old, although this was a condition that was later lifted. In fact the youngest recorded u-boat commander, Ludwig-Ferdinand von Friedeburg, was just twenty years and three months old when he became a u-boat commander in mid-August 1944. The upper limit for a u-boat commander was set at around forty years. Most of the men in this photograph, particularly the crew themselves, would have been between seventeen and twenty three years old. Parental consent was required to serve for any man under the age of twenty one.

This photograph shows four members of the U-108 crew, which was presumably taken in December 1940. From left to right, marked 1 to 4, are Rudolf-Georg Treu, who was then a boson. Treu was born in July 1909 and died on September 28 1944 at Bordeaux. The second man is motor man Staplemann of which very little is known. The third man is navigator Albert Dahlmann. He had previously served on the U-10 and was the brother of Kurt Dahlmann, who served on the U-100. The fourth man is identified as being motor man Warne. It is possible that this man is in fact Heinrich Warner, as he is not listed as being a member of the U-108 crew but instead is listed as part of the U-191 crew. The entire crew of the U-191 was lost on April 23 1943 when it was depth charged by HMS *Hesperus* and HMS *Clematis* off Cape Farewell, Greenland.

This is a portrait of Klaus Scholtz, who was born in Magdeburg on March 22 1908. When this photograph was taken he was just thirty two years old. He was already a Kapitan-Leutnant, having risen to this rank in October 1936. Scholtz would have a successful career onboard the U-108 and, as we will see, during his first patrol, which began in February 1941, the U-108 would sink two enemy vessels with a combined tonnage of some 8,000tons.

Chapter 2

The Commander

Klaus Scholtz was one of fourteen men that were part of Crew 27; an intake of officers, all of which would go on to command u-boats. Although records are often contradictory, Klaus Scholtz and the U-108 are credited with around twenty five sinkings of Allied ships. The first took place on February 22 1941, when the Dutch steam merchant ship, *Texelstroom,* was sunk *en route* from Reykjavik to Grimsby just after 2200 hours. The U-108 hit it with a torpedo and the ship changed course. At 2246 a second torpedo was fired, which exploded prematurely. A third torpedo hit the vessel and it sank within three minutes. It is believed that some of the crew managed to scramble aboard lifeboats. There was very poor visibility and snow was falling; none of the crew survived.

The last recorded vessel sunk by Scholtz was the American motor tanker, *Louisiana,* which was travelling between Trinidad and Rio de Janeiro in Brazil. It was unescorted and the U-108 fired three torpedoes at it. At least one of the torpedoes hit the *Louisiana,* but she still tried to escape. Scholtz ordered the U-108 to surface and fire at her with a deck gun. The Norwegian merchant ship, *Tercero,* tried to get between the *Louisiana* and the U-108. This gave the *Louisiana* a chance to try and escape. Shortly before 2300 hours Scholtz was forced to order the U-108 to dive when an aircraft appeared and dropped a bomb. He then manoeuvred the U-108 and fired two more torpedoes at the *Louisiana,* both of which hit her shortly before midnight on August 17 1942. She sank with the loss of forty nine crewmembers.

This is a photograph from the album, but it appears to have been clipped from a contemporary newspaper or magazine. It shows Scholtz, presumably post-late December 1941, as he has his Knight's Cross around his neck. The official title of this award was the Knight's Cross of the Iron Cross. It was an award for extreme bravery or leadership. The award goes back to the beginning of the nineteenth century, when the Prussians established the Iron Cross to reflect military gallantry and defiance against Napoleon. The Iron Cross, as a Second World War award, was brought back in September 1939. It had been awarded for gallantry during the First World War. The Knight's Cross was very similar in appearance to the Iron Cross. They were manufactured in silver and this was the first of five grades of the Knight's Cross. The most prestigious was the Knight's Cross of the Iron Cross with Golden Oak Leaves, Swords and Diamonds. During the war some 7,313 individuals were awarded the Knight's Cross. Scholtz was one of 883 to receive the Oak Leaves. This was essentially a clasp, which was awarded for leadership, gallantry and distinguished service. Many of the oak leaf awards were presented to the recipients by Hitler himself.

This is another slightly enhanced photograph of Scholtz, presumably taken for propaganda purposes. At this stage in his career Scholtz had attained the rank of Kapitan-Leutnant. Having served in the Kriegsmarine since 1927, he had attained this rank by October 1936. It is not possible to see the shoulder straps in this photograph, although they would have probably been plain with two stars to denote his rank. The cap Scholtz is wearing is known as a Schirmmutze, or visor cap. It was the regulation service dress headgear. The blue cap was worn by all officer ranks but unofficially a white top would be added, however this was usually only worn whilst at sea. It had a broad band of gold embroidered oak leaves on the peak. This type of visor cap would be worn up to the grade of Kapitan-Leutnant.

Scholtz's previous command was the torpedo boat, *Jaguar*, which he commanded between June 3 1937 and April 1939. The *Jaguar* had been built at Wilhelmshaven in May 1937. She would have a varied career during the course of the Second World War. By the time the Allies landed in Normandy in June 1944 the vessel was based at Le Havre. The Allies launched a concerted effort to destroy German naval forces at the base on June 14 and it is believed that the *Jaguar* was hit at least four times by bombs dropped by Lancasters and that she sank with the loss of sixteen of her crew.

This photograph shows the radio operator, Bruno Aniszewski, giving Klaus Scholtz a haircut onboard the U-108. Aniszewski was an Oberfunkmaat, part of the radio section onboard the u-boat. It is believed that he was born on March 26 1919 and that he served with the U-108 and subsequently with the U-960 and the U-968. Onboard the last vessel Aniszewski was present for the first eight of fifteen active operations, which took place between January 1943 and May 1945. He was awarded the German Cross in Gold on March 11 1945.

A relaxed shot of Scholtz wearing his sunglasses and smoking a cigar can be seen here, which suggest that this photograph was taken in one of the later patrols in the South Atlantic. In each of the first three patrols the U-108 managed to sink Allied shipping. It was unsuccessful in its fourth active patrol, but for its fifth, sixth, seventh and eighth enemy vessels became victim of this increasingly tight group and experienced commander. The eighth sailing, which took place between July 13 1942 and September 10 1942, was the last under the command of Scholtz. Presumably this was also the point at which Willi Wilke left the vessel. His album suggests that he was not part of the U-108 crew when Ralf-Reimar Wolfram took command of the u-boat for his first mission with her, leaving Lorient on October 25 1942. Immediately after the command of U-108 Klaus Scholtz became commander of the 12th Flotilla in Bordeaux. This photograph may well have been taken on one of his last two patrols, which were in Caribbean and US waters.

Life onboard a u-boat was claustrophobic, even for the captain of the vessel. The seamen would work in three, eight-hour shifts. One of the shifts was for sleeping, the second for regular duties and the third for other tasks. Radio men would have three, four-hour shifts, between 0800 and 2000 and two, six-hour shifts during the night. Even for the captain accommodation was at a premium; most of the men had a simple locker for their personal effects. It was only when some torpedoes had been fired that there was additional space for some of the crewmen to put their bunks or hammocks. As can be seen in this photograph, privacy was virtually unknown. Even the officers' bunks were laid out either side of a busy walkway down the centre of the vessel. The captain's quarters would be separated from the rest of the boat by a curtain. Like other captains, Scholtz's quarters were near the control room and the radio room, so that he could be called to post if there were an emergency of any kind.

Chapter 3

The Crew

The number of crew members obviously depended on the size of the vessel. A typical Type IX u-boat, like the U-108, would have around fifty crewmembers. Smaller Type II u-boats had just twenty five and the Type XXI had fifty seven.

The u-boat crew had a typical command structure, consisting of a number of officers, chief petty officers, petty officers and seamen. Although the four officers had overall responsibility for the vessel, it was largely the chief petty officers and petty officers that carried out the bulk of the day to day work. There were usually four chief petty officers.

The boson (Oberbootsmann) was responsible for crew discipline. The navigator (Obersteuermann) was not only responsible for navigation but also for supplies. There were two further chief petty officers that worked under the command of the leading engineer (Leitender Ingenieur); one handled the diesel engines (Diesel Obermaschinist) and the other the batteries and electric motors (Electro Obermaschinist).

Reporting to the chief petty officers were the petty officers. There would be a number of these men, perhaps as many as one for every two or three ordinary seamen. They tended to work in five main areas; the Maschinisten were responsible for the engines, the Mechaniker for the torpedoes, the Steuermann for the steering, the Bootsmanner for discipline and supervising the rest of the crew and the Funkmaat for sound equipment and radio communication.

The rest of the men all had specific duties and they were known as Matrosen, or seamen. It was these individuals that handled the day to day operations, such as dealing with the torpedoes, preparing food, manning the deck guns or carrying out maintenance or watches on the deck.

Just as any branch of the armed services are concerned, there was a strict hierarchy. The engine room would have a Diesel Obermaschinist 1, an Electro Obermaschinist 1 and then, depending on the size of the boat, a number of diesel and electro machinists. Even within this small part of the crew there would be a number of ranks, from Obermaschinistmaat to Maschinistmaat and then Maschinisthauptgefrieter, Maschinistobergefrieter and Maschinistgefrieter.

The general seaman ranks included Matrosenhauptgefrieter, Matrosenobergefrieter, Matrosengefrieter and Matrosen.

As far as the officers were concerned, the commander of the u-boat would tend to be a Kapitan Leutnant. His first watch officer would be an Oberleutnant zur See, the second watch officer a Leutnant zur See. It was also likely that there would be officer cadets of midshipmen onboard. This would usually mean two cadets, one of which would be an Oberfahnrich zur See and the other a Fahnrich zur See.

Otto Fechner in shown in this photograph; he served on the U-108, probably between March and October of 1941. Fechner was born in November 1905, near Posen and had joined the German navy in 1924 and had already attained the rank of Kapitan Leutnant before the outbreak of the Second World War. He was a highly decorated individual, winning the Iron Cross Second Class in 1939, the Iron Cross First Class in 1940, the Fleet War Badge in October 1941 and the U-Boat War Badge in 1942. Fechner would go on to command the U-164 and claim three vessels. On his first patrol with the U-164, which left Kiel in July 1942 and returned to Lorient at the beginning of the October, he sank the Dutch *Stad Amsterdam* on August 25. This was a cargo steamer that had been built in 1920 and she was *en route* from Liverpool to America, carrying freight and bags of mail. On September 6 1942 the U-164 sank the *John A Holloway*, which was heading from Florida to Trinidad, carrying construction equipment. On his second patrol, which left Lorient on November 29 1942, the U-164 sank the *Brageland* on New Year's Day 1943. This was a Swedish vessel *en route* from Buenos Aires to America, carrying coffee, cheese and wool, along with mail. This would be the last victim of the U-164; she was found by a US Catalina in the south Atlantic on January 6 1943. Depth charges destroyed the U-164 and only two of the fifty six crewmembers onboard this Type IXC submarine survived and Fechner was not one of them. Interestingly, Fechner had the rank of Korvetten Kapitan, which he had achieved in August 1939.

This photograph shows Paul Karl Loeser and a crewman believed to be named Friedrichs in extremely inclement weather, probably off Iceland. Kapitan Leutnant Loeser was the first officer onboard the U-108 and at this time he was an Oberleutnant zur See. Loeser was born in Berlin on April 26 1915. He had already had a wide ranging career in u-boats before he joined the U-108. He had been the second officer onboard the U-33 in March 1938, had held the same rank onboard the U-40 between February and September 1939 and had become the first officer onboard the U-43 between September 1939 and July 1940. He joined the U-108 in October 1940 and remained with her for only a short time, until March 1941. Loeser then went on to become the acting commander of the U-30 in April 1941. At this time the U-30 did not undertake any active combat patrols. By May 1941 Loeser had taken command of the U-373, remaining with this vessel until September 1943. He had graduated as a u-boat officer in 1935.

It is his service onboard the U-373 for which he is most known, with three ships sunk in March and June 1942. At this stage the U-373 was operating out of La Pallice. On March 17 1942 the U-373 sunk the Greek steam merchant ship, *Mount Lycabettus*, which was bound for Portugal from Baltimore carrying wheat. All thirty of the crew perished. Five days later, on March 22, the U-373 sunk the British vessel *Thursobank*. On June 24 the U-373 claimed the American steam tug *John R Williams*, which was bound for New Jersey. She hit a mine, one of fifteen that had been laid by the U-373, and sank with the loss of fourteen of its eighteen crewmembers.

The U-373 was attacked on three occasions during Loeser's command. She narrowly avoided destruction by depth charges on August 25 1942, an attack by a US Liberator on March 2 1943 and a further attack by US aircraft off Portugal on July 24 1943. Loeser survived the war and died at the age of seventy one, in 1987.

This photograph shows the second watch officer, Heinz Konrad Fenn. He would go on to command the U-139 and the U-445. Fenn served onboard the U-108 between October 1940 and July 1941. He took over command of the U-139 in the October remaining with her until May 1942. In the May he assumed command of U-445 and remained in this post until January 1944. We know that he left the U-445 and was hospitalised from February to March 1944.

Fenn was born on July 20 1918 and had joined the German navy, graduating as an officer in 1937. By the time he joined the U-108 he was a Leutnant, having achieved this rank in August 1939. In September 1941 he became an Oberleutnant and attained the rank of Kapitan Leutnant in August 1944.

This is a second photograph of Oberleutnant Fenn manning one of the U-108's machine guns. Fenn was awarded the Iron Cross Second Class on March 13 1941. He attained his u-boat war badge in May of the same year and the Iron Cross First Class in 1942. Directly after his service on U-108 Fenn took command of the U-139, a Type IID submarine. This vessel did not have any combat patrols during his period as commander. When he assumed command of the U-445, a Type VIIC submarine, he was to accompany it for five patrols, from November 1942 to January 1944. From February 1942 the U-445 was stationed at St Nazaire. The U-445 is not credited with the sinking of any ships, however the patrols were not without incident and the U-445 was also involved in a number of Wolfpack operations. During Fenn's patrol that left St Nazaire on February 7 1943 the U-445 was out for nearly seven weeks, coming under attack from an unidentified aircraft.

Oberleutnant Fenn can be seen in this shot, together with Willi Keull, who was an Obermaschinist, inside the U-108. Very little is known about Willi Keull, beyond the fact that he served on the U-108. As far as Fenn was concerned, when he was onboard the U-445 on January 2 1944, he survived an attack in the north Atlantic by a Halifax bomber of RAF 58 Squadron. The Halifax dropped around five depth charges, badly wounding one of the u-boat crew and inflicting some damage on the vessel. The damage could not have been overly significant, however, as the u-boat managed to get back to St Nazaire on January 10.

After Fenn had left the U-445 the submarine continued operations, but she was sunk to the west of St Nazaire, in the Bay of Biscay, by HMS *Louis* on August 24 1944. The entire crew of fifty two men were killed.

This is a photograph of Oberleutnant Herbert Neckel, who had been born in Kiel in 1916. He had graduated as an officer in the German navy in April 1935 and his first active posting was onboard the U-30, as first officer, between September 1940 and March 1941. Neckel joined the U-108 in March 1941, remaining with her until the November of the same year. By this stage he was an Oberleutnant, having attained this rank in October 1939.

Neckel would go on to command the U-531 from October 1942 to his death on May 6 1943.

A second photograph of Herbert Neckel can be seen here. He took over command of the U-531 in October 1942. His one and only patrol began on April 13 1943 out of Kiel. He was bound for the u-boat hunting grounds off Canada in the north Atlantic. The u-boat was first attacked by a Catalina belonging to RAF 190 Squadron on April 22 and then by a second aircraft, believed to be a Flying Fortress of RAF 206 Squadron. Both aircraft were operating out of Iceland. It was originally believed that the U-531, a Type IXC submarine, had been sunk by HMS *Oribi,* a destroyer and the Corvette HMS *Snowflake.* But in actual fact the submarine that they had destroyed was the U-125. The U-531 was in fact destroyed by depth charges to the northeast of Newfoundland on exactly the same day, May 6, but by HMS *Vidette.* All fifty four members of the u-boat crew, including Neckel, were killed. The U-531 was aiming to join up with the Wolfpack operation Fink (or Finch). It was a fairly disastrous operation for the Germans, as on the night of May 5 to 6 five u-boats, including the U-531, were lost. The others lost during this operation were the U-125, U-192, U-438, and U-630.

This is a photograph of Obersteuermann I (Chief Navigator) Albert Dahlmann, using his sextant. Many of the sextants were made by the manufacturer Plath in Hamburg. They would come complete with accessories and were stored in a wooden box. The sextants were vital to ensure correct positioning. The navigator would need to be extremely skilled in the use of the sextant and may only have had a matter of minutes to confirm the u-boat's position, particularly in water where the u-boat was likely to be spotted by enemy aircraft.

Another photograph of Obersteuermann I Albert Dahlmann can be seen here. He was the brother of Kurt Dahlmann, who served onboard the U-100. Kurt Dahlmann was a Maschinistobergefrieter and a member of the engine room crew. The U-100 was a Type VIIB submarine. Kurt was extremely fortunate when the U-100 was rammed and then depth charged by HMS *Walker* and HMS *Vanoc* to the southeast of Iceland in the early hours of the morning on March 17 1941. Of the forty four crew onboard the U-100, commanded by Kapitan Leutnant Joachim Schepke, Kurt was one of only six survivors. He was to spend the rest of the conflict as a prisoner of war.

Albert Dahlmann is seen here using his sextant in the conning tower of the U-108. Plath had been making sextants in Hamburg since the middle of the nineteenth century. In the immediate aftermath of the Second World War the company was virtually dismantled, with much of its production equipment being shipped east into Soviet Russia. It was not until 1950 that they began producing sextants again, along with other nautical equipment. The company changed hands several times in the 1960s through to the 1990s. What remains of the company is now a part of the Northrop Grumman Corporation.

This photograph shows Obermaschinistmaat Heinz Ackermann. Unfortunately little is known about this particular individual, apart from the fact that he served onboard the U-108, as part of the engine room crew. It is unclear whether he remained with the U-108 throughout its active service career, which ran from October 1940 through to April 1944. If he did so, he would have served under four different u-boat commanders; initially Klaus Scholtz, who was replaced by Oberleutnant Erich Hilsenitz. His command was restricted just to a matter of hours in October 1942 when Korvettenkapitan Ralf-Reimar Wolfram remained with the vessel until October 16 1943. The final commander was Oberleutnant Matthias Brűnig.

This is a second photograph of Obermaschinistmaat Heinz Ackermann. This time he appears to be wearing a Kriegsmarine leather u-boat jacket and a singularly unofficial woollen hat. This was somewhat different from the black leather coat that was worn by commanders and officers, which were mainly worn during poor weather patrols in the Atlantic and the Bay of Biscay. Ackermann is wearing the standard leather jacket that was issued to engine room personnel. It was single-breasted and had barely changed in terms of design since the First World War. Many of the jackets were actually made from goats' skin rather than horse hide.

Willi Wilke can be seen here, undergoing a ritual involving King Neptune as the U-108 crosses the equator for the first time. Rituals differed from vessel to vessel but usually involved cracking eggs on their heads, covering in shaving foam and otherwise humiliating the victims that were crossing the equator for the first time. This was a tradition that had gone back for decades as far as mariners were concerned. All officers and sailors who had not yet crossed the equator had to be initiated into the mysteries and to enter the dominion of Neptune. In earlier times this could be something of a brutal event, which could involve the victims being thrown over the side of the ship and dragged by a rope from the stern.

This photograph shows Oberbootsmann Hans Begale in an impromptu bath tub on the deck of the U-108. Cleanliness was extremely important, as fresh water was limited and only ever used for drinking. Sometimes even fresh water would be so limited, as water tanks were often filled with diesel fuel to extend the operational range. Under normal circumstances there would be no showers or baths, hence the novel use of seawater in this case. The crews were issued with special saltwater soap to remove salt from their skin, but this was extremely unpopular as it left a film on the skin's surface.

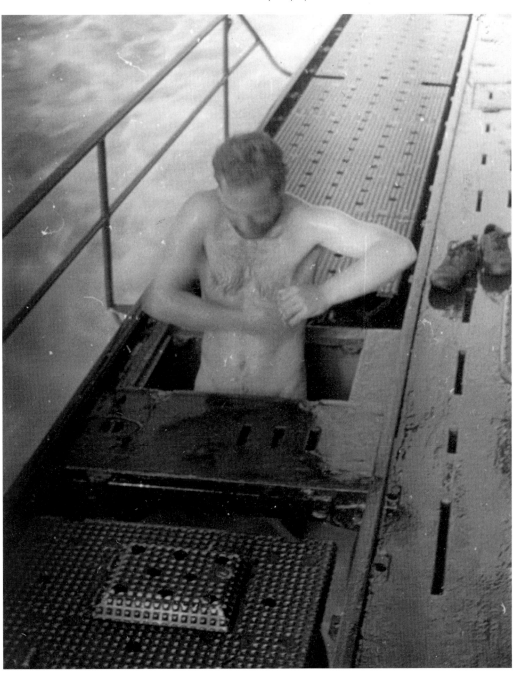

This shot shows Bootsmann Heinrich Behrens. The photograph indicates that Behrens is involved in using the navigation charts on what is called a switching table. Basically it was a card table that used protractors and rulers that could be used for nautical charts. It was vital that the submarine's position was always known and equally as important that navigation ensured the safest and most efficient way to get from one position to another. We have already seen the use of the sextant as a tool for surface navigation. Using the navigation charts tended to be used for underwater navigation. The submarine's position was determined by the crossing of at least two lines of position. In many cases the submarine crew had to use dead reckoning navigation. It would have to be based on a precise fixed position that noted the submarine's course, which was drawn on the nautical chart plus the submarine's speed and the elapsed time. This should give the new position of the submarine. However this was not a precise science, as the sea current could affect the distance that had been travelled, and indeed the direction in which the submarine had been travelling.

Heinrich Behrens is seen again in this photograph, this time manning the rear rudder. In fact this was the rudder that was used to control the hydroplane, which was used for the fine control and rotation of the u-boat when it was submerged. The hydroplane, or deep rudder, was mounted at the rear of the u-boat and was used to fine tune the movement of the submarine whilst underwater. Tiefenruder literally means low rudder.

Two members of the crew are seen here, but unfortunately they have not been positively identified, although one of the men may be Maschinistgerfrieter Johann Siano. He was born on February 21 1920 and died during an air raid on Wilhelmshaven on January 15 1941. The photograph description also seems to indicate that these two men were involved in the gunnery section of the U-108, which contradicts the rank of Siano. The gunnery section would be responsible for the on deck weaponry, which would include anti-aircraft guns and deck guns. The latter would often be used to finish off crippled or abandoned enemy vessels. Bearing in mind that on long patrols torpedoes would be limited in supply, and that the torpedoes were not necessarily guaranteed to sink an enemy merchant ship, the crew often had to resort to using the deck guns in order to finish the victim off. If the submarine was caught above surface by an enemy aircraft the only immediate defensive armament was anti-aircraft guns. These would be used to hold off the enemy aircraft until the last possible moment, as the u-boat submerged and tried to get into deep water to avoid the inevitable depth charge attacks.

We can see here a photograph of Matrosenobergefrieter Richard Käufer. Multi-skilling onboard the u-boat was extremely important. The most important asset of a submarine was not to be seen until it had launched an attack and then to be able to withdraw as quickly as possible to avoid detection. All crew members had to be alert and capable of performing a wide variety of different duties. The men could find themselves assigned to various parts of the vessel, undertaking different roles.

Scholtz is seen in this photograph, supervising a crash dive, which the photograph states is a dive of 30m in 25 seconds. Evasive tactics were the best defence if the u-boat was spotted on the surface. Obviously enemy aircraft would try to drop depth charges, as would escort shipping. Escort ships were also not averse to ramming the u-boat. The u-boat would normally need around 30 seconds to crash dive to a safe enough depth to evade depth charges. Hence the timing, set at 25 seconds, shows a proficient crew of the U-108.

This is a photograph of Kapitan Leutnant Hermann Schmidt, who was the fourth officer onboard the U-108, as he was the chief engineer. Ensuring the smooth running of a submarine was a twenty four hour a day job whilst it was on patrol. The Type IX was designed to be a long-range weapon and they had to be able to operate in relatively distant waters. The U-108, as one of these submarine types, had to be able to travel to its area of operations as quickly as possible, whilst carrying enough torpedoes and stores to make a valuable effort and contribution each time it set out to sea. It had large and powerful diesel engines, which were supercharged 9 cylinder models. The Type IX, in its various forms, was the backbone of the German u-boat force. Across the different variants some 200 Type IXs were built. There were in fact seven sub-classes. The Type IXB had a fuel capacity of around 165tons, which gave it a range of some 8,700 nautical miles.

Schmidt would go on to serve on the U-3032, which was commissioned on February 12 1945 and, under the command of Oberleutnant Horst Slevogt. The U-3032 did not undertake any active war patrols, as it was still in training in May 1945 when it was sunk by rockets fired by a Typhoon of RAF 184 Squadron to the east of the German island of Fehmarn. Thirty six of the crew were killed and there were twenty four survivors.

The photograph caption suggests that this is Maschinistmaat Kampf in the engine control room of the U-108. Several men with the surname Kampf served on a number of different u-boats during the Second World War, although none are directly linked to the U-108. Two likely candidates, however, were both lost in 1943, Johannes when the U-467 was lost to the southeast of Iceland and Helmut, who was lost when the U-634 went down to the east of the Azores.

This photograph shows Georg Malinthki. He is noted in the photograph album as being an Obergerfieter in the radio section of the U-108. A vital part of the job of crewmen like Malinthki was to use the radio detection finder. Radio detection finders were fitted onto German submarines and consisted of a receiver and an antenna. This made it possible for them to determine the direction of enemy vessels. A second job was to operate underground sound detection devices. This had been developed since the First World War and now consisted of an acoustic system, a compensator, an amplifier and indicator. The submarine could work out the average distance between it and an enemy vessel. The sound detection equipment worked better and was more accurate and longer-ranged if the submarine was either stationary or barely moving. As the war progressed active sonar or Asdic was fitted to Allied vessels, particularly escorts, which made it increasingly more difficult for the submarine to remain undetected.

This is a photograph of Kurt Patz, although he is otherwise listed as Karl Patz. He was also involved in the radio section on the U-108. Each of the u-boats was given an enigma machine, which was effectively a cipher machine that allowed them to send and receive messages in code. All u-boats used the Dolphin naval enigma cipher at the beginning of the war. The code was broken by the British at the beginning of August 1941. Vessels such as the U-108 then used the Shark cipher from the beginning of October 1941, which was used until the beginning of February 1942.

Here we can see Obermaschinistmaat Hans Simon. Again very little is known about this particular individual, only that he served onboard the U-108 at the same time as Willi Wilke. Simon's clothing may suggest that he was involved in engine room duties.

These crewmen are being awarded the EKII U-Boat Badge. In effect this was of course the Iron Cross Second Class. Presumably this ceremony took place at the end of one of the U-108's operations during Wilke's service on the vessel. It is likely, therefore, that this was a direct result of these crewmembers' work, perhaps during the third active patrol, which took place between May 25 and July 7 1941. This was when the U-108 sank seven enemy vessels. Noted as recipients in the photograph album are Willi Keull, and Heinz-Hugo Lehmann, who we know was born in Dresden in September 1915. This was his second submarine posting; as he had already served onboard the U-32 and would go on to serve on the U-1228, which was commissioned in December 1943. It undertook its first operation in September 1944 and claimed its only victim, HMCS *Shawinigan*, on November 25 1944.

All we know about this individual is that he was an Obermaschinistmaat called Zimmer. There was another similarly named Bootsmaat, Harry Zimmermann, onboard the U-108 and this individual later went on to serve on the U-123 and the U-124.

Signalling from the conning tower of the U-108 can be seen in this shot, whilst it is docked alongside another vessel in an unknown port. In order to operate the signal lamp a cable had to be extended through the hatch. The lamp bulbs were not designed for high shock usage and if the vessel was attacked by depth charges it was likely that most of the bulbs would be broken. The sight signalling apparatus included two signal searchlights, one Morse lamp, signal and semaphore flags, a signal pistol and fireworks.

A group of crewmen are enjoying beer on the deck of the U-108 in this photograph. The superstructure of the submarine consisted of a fairly light frame of plates. The remainder of the deck was made up of slatted wood. There were a number of openings in the hull; two were torpedo hatches, another for the galley, one for the engine room and an opening in the control room for the conning tower hatch and the two periscopes.

One of the crewmembers is playing the accordion on the deck of the U-108 here, next to one of the deck guns. The deck gun is positioned forward of the conning tower and had a heavy cast ring for the mounting bolts. Ladders were arranged to enable rapid descent from the bridge to the control room and from the bridge to the deck guns. There were special storage lockers for deck gear in the superstructure. Lockers were also placed adjacent to the deck gun and to the machine guns on the bridge. The pressure proof tanks next to the deck gun could hold around thirty two rounds and an additional 218 rounds were stowed in two magazine spaces below deck.

Four of the officers and crew are posing on the conning tower in this photograph. Note the icicles hanging from the hand rails and wiring. Under battle station conditions there would be four men stationed in the conning tower. Normally, when surfaced, three crewmen would be considered to be sufficient. The conning tower had two loudspeakers, a pair of microphones connected in parallel and a connection box for connecting a portable microphone and headset. There was a voice tube system used for communication to allow communication between the sound room, the radio room and the conning tower. This was achieved by means of a flexible metal hose.

Members of the crew in extreme conditions are wearing their cold weather, waterproof uniforms. Note the radio and radar equipment shown in this photograph. These types of submarine would have a 20W radio transmitter, a 150W radio transmitter, a shortwave receiver, a broadcast radio receiver, a second shortwave radio receiver and radar surface search equipment. It would also have a radio direction finder. It would have two antennae for the radar, one of which would be stored as a spare.

Crewmembers are on watch in the conning tower in this shot. Note the flexible hose pipe running from the conning tower for voice communication. There were in fact fewer berths than crewmen onboard; hence some of the berths had to be shared, which was achieved by men alternating on watches. The crew quarters were located in the forward and after torpedo rooms. In the forward torpedo room there were ten folding berths and twenty eight lockers. In the after torpedo room there were eight folding berths and eighteen lockers. The berths had spring bottoms with spring cushions. The petty officers' quarters had eight berths and a further twenty six lockers. The commanding officer had a state room, which boasted a book shelf that doubled as a locker, desk and washstand. He also had an upholstered stool with stowage for papers.

Two crewmembers are featured in this photograph, in the conning tower whilst the U-108 is in port. Both of the men are wearing simple Kriegsmarine side caps. These caps were often referred to as the bordmutz.

An alternative version of headgear can be seen in this photograph; this time, a fur-lined cap with ear protectors. Even in reasonable weather, standing for hours and keeping an alert watch from the conning tower would be an onerous task and ear protection such as this would have been vital.

This image shows Kapitan Leutnant Schmidt, the leading engineer. The handwritten caption on the photograph seems to imply that Schmidt did not survive the war and died as a result of a brain tumour.

Obermaschinist Heinz Stapelmann is another crew member of whom we know very little, other than the fact that he was on the U-108 during the time Wilke served on her. It is clear from his title that he was involved in engine room work, however. Stapelmann is wearing the u-boat battle dress made of leather and another non-regulation hat. Under normal circumstances he would be wearing the schiffchen, or forage cap.

A characterful shot of Rudolf-Georg Treu, who was a senior ordinary seaman onboard the U-108. Many of the crewmen were specialists, working in the engine room, on the torpedoes or in the radio room. They would tend to sleep one shift and then carry out regular duties for another and miscellaneous tasks for the third. All ranks would be entitled to a bronze u-boat war badge, which had been introduced in 1939, provided they had served on two active patrols or had been wounded in action.

A perplexing photograph here, showing Obermaschinistmaat Jack Kämpf. He does not appear on the crew records for the U-108, but this does not necessarily mean that he was not assigned to that particular submarine. It may merely infer that he was either only with the U-108 for a short period of time, or that he was assigned to another vessel before the U-108 went out on any active service patrols. Having searched through u-boat crew lists, no record of a Jack Kämpf can be found related to any u-boats. Again this is not unusual, as crew records were often lost or names mis-transcribed.

This is a posed photograph of Obermaschinistmaat Willi Keull. Little is known about Keull's service record beyond the fact that he served on the U-108.

Obermaschinistmaat Werner Todt is featured in this photograph. Todt had previously served on the Type IIB submarine, the U-17. This vessel had been commissioned in 1935. We do not know Todt's age or how long he had been in the German navy. We must presume, however, that he had joined the U-108 at some point on or after October 1940. The U-17 had already undertaken at least five active patrols before October 1940. Its most successful patrol took place between February 29 1940 and March 7 1940. The submarine had left Wilhelmshaven under the command of Udo Behrens. They encountered two Dutch vessels, sinking them both. The *Rijnstroom* was sunk on March 2 and the *Grutto* on March 5. The ultimate fate of the U-17 was that she was scuttled on May 4 1945, having been decommissioned in February of that year.

In cold weather gear, with sunglasses, this photograph shows Oberbootsmann, or warrant officer Max Henke. He was born in 1914 and served onboard the U-26, U-139 and the U-196, as well as the U-108. It is believed that Henke was onboard the U-196 when she went down near the Sunda Straits, to the south of Java on December 1 1944. In command was Oberleutnant Werner Striegler. This was Striegler's first patrol with the U-196. Throughout the war the U-196 had sunk three enemy vessels. In March 1944 the vessel left La Pallice and arrived in Penang on August 10. On September 1 it went on a one-day sea trial and left for its first active sea patrol in the Far East on November 30, where it went down with the loss of all sixty five members of the crew. The vessel was a Type IXD2.

This photograph features Oberbootsmann Heinrich Behrens. Effectively he was a chief petty officer and although responsible for crew discipline, he was likely to have had his own particular specialism either as an electrical or mechanical engineer.

Oberbootsmann Hans Begale is wearing waterproofs and a sou'wester and is pictured in this photograph with his binoculars in the conning tower of the U-108.

Members of the crew and officers are on deck in this photograph. Note the second unidentified German submarine alongside the U-108. The majority of the men are wearing their work overalls, which were one-piece garments, whilst the remainder are wearing their duty uniforms. Note that several of the crew are wearing gloves, which infers that they were doing heavy hauling or rope work.

The U-108 is alongside a ship in dock in this picture. Note the wooden gangplank in the foreground. The men are wearing a variety of Kriegsmarine uniforms, mostly work gear, although the officer to the right of the photograph seems to be in full dress uniform.

Five officers and crew are in the conning tower here. They are adopting battle stations watch. Note that the three men using binoculars are scanning the horizon in different directions. It was essential for the u-boat to ensure that it was not caught unawares. An enemy aircraft could appear suddenly in the distance and the submarine may only have a matter of seconds to submerge before coming under attack. It was therefore essential to have the maximum amount of warning.

This photograph shows Kapitan Leutnant Scholtz in the conning tower of the U-108. Note that he is wearing a white cover over the top of his cap. He has his characteristic, several weeks' growth of beard. This may suggest that the photograph was taken when the U-108 was returning to port after one of its active patrols.

This is a very clear picture of the cramped conditions, even in the control room of the U-108. Also visible in the background of the photograph is the entrance to the next compartment of the vessel. The steering arrangements for a Type IX submarine consisted of twin rudders. There were electric steering stations in the control room and the conning tower. The main operating stations were located in the control room. There was a voice tube direct from the bridge to the conning tower and to the control room. The control room was amidships, within the pressure hull of the vessel. There was a steering station, normal plain control stations, a chart board and locker, depth gauges, snorkel extension indicator, magnetic compass, sound powered telephones and a host of other indicators and panels. When the submarine was on the surface five men would work in the control room. There would be ten if the submarine was at battle stations.

One of the crewmen is manning the rear rudder controls in this photograph. More accurately, this is the planes man station. These men were known as ruderganger. In order to make the U-108 dive the forward plane would have to be tilted down and the aft plane up. Under normal circumstances the chief engineer would direct operations. If the u-boat was under threat, regardless of whether they were on duty or not, the most experienced planes men would man the stations. The large dials above the station are the depth meter and the gauge that shows the periscope elevation. The two operators would sit on seats in front of the controls. There are large buttons close to the large wheels, which operated the plane via an electric motor.

Willi Wilke and a man identified in the album as Alleweld are featured in this photograph. The only reference to a man called Alleweld is a Helmut Alleweld, who was a maschinistobergerfrieter. He was born in February 1921. Research does not indicate that he had a long-term association with the U-108 but instead he is believed to have been a crewman onboard the Type VIIC, U-375. It is perfectly possible that he was transferred to this vessel when it was commissioned in mid-July 1941. What we do know is that the U-375 was sunk in the Mediterranean, to the north of Malta, by the American submarine chaser USS *PC624* on July 30 1943. In its two year career the U-375 sank nine vessels and damaged a warship. When she was sunk in July 1943 she had carried out eleven patrols, but she went down with all forty six hands lost.

Chapter 4

The U-Boat

The U-108 undertook eleven active patrols. From the outset the vessel and its commander and crew proved to be extremely successful. The first active patrol took place out of Wilhelmshaven on February 15 1941. They returned three and a half weeks later, on March 12, having sunk two vessels. As we will see when we look at the *Effna* photographs in Chapter 6, there is some debate as to whether these photographs, or indeed the fate of the *Effna* are correctly detailed.

What we do know, however, is that on this first active patrol the U-108 sank the Dutch steam freighter *Texelstroom* on February 22 1941, at approximately 2224 hours. She is believed to have been sunk by torpedoes and that the crew were all lost. The Dutch vessel had been making its way from Reykjavik, which it had left on February 12, bound for Grimsby.

On February 28 the U-108 sank the former American-built steam freighter *Effna* at 2332 hours. The vessel was carrying steel and trucks from out of Baltimore and Halifax, bound for Newport. She had been built in 1919 and her crew of thirty three were all presumed lost.

On the U-108's second active patrol, which began on April 3 1941 and lasted until May 2, she attacked Convoy HX117. Her victim was the armed merchant cruiser HMS *Rajputana*. Again the attack was by torpedo and this time the attack came in at 0743 on April 13. Forty of the crew were lost.

The U-108's most successful active patrol was its third one. This began on May 25 1941 and was to last for six weeks, during which time she managed to sink seven Allied vessels. The first victim was the *Michael E*, which was a British steam freighter heading out of Belfast bound for Halifax. She was torpedoed on June 2 at 2043 hours and four of her sixty four crewmembers were killed.

The next victim was the *Baron Nairn* that was a part of Convoy OB-328. This attack took place on June 8 1941. The steam freighter had left Barrow and was heading for Nueveitas in Cuba. She too was torpedoed and one of the forty man-crew was killed.

On the same day the U-108 also sunk the Greek steam freighter *Dirphys*, which was carrying coal out of Swansea and bound for Montreal. The torpedo attack took place just after 0600 hours and six of the crew were killed with nineteen later picked up.

Two days later the U-108 sank the Norwegian vessel *Christian Crohg*. She was a steam freighter that had left London and had then travelled to Oban in Scotland and was bound for Pointe-au-Pere (Father Point), at the mouth of the St Lawrence River in Canada. It was a torpedo attack that took place at 0723 and twenty three of the crew were lost. The Norwegian vessel had been part of Convoy OB-239.

On June 25 1941 the U-108 sank two Greek vessels; the *Ellinico,* which was a steam freighter that had been built in 1904. She had left the Liverpool area on June 14 and was headed for Wabana, on Bell Island, in the province of Newfoundland and Labrador. The U-108 torpedoed her at 0620 hours. It is not clear whether the crewmembers were killed in this attack. At 1614 hours the U-108 torpedoed the Greek steam freighter *Nicolas Pateras,* which had been built in 1910. She had headed out from Liverpool, bound for Father Point. All those onboard were lost.

The final victim of this very successful patrol for the U-108 was claimed on July 1 1941. This was the British steam freighter built in 1925 called *Toronto City.* She was headed for Newfoundland and was torpedoed at 1825 hours. It is presumed that the crew of forty four men were lost.

By this stage the U-108 was operating out of Lorient. In fact she had been using this as her main base since her second active patrol. The U-108 left for its fourth patrol on August 19 1941 and returned empty-handed on October 21. She was more fortunate on her fifth active patrol however, which began on December 9 and lasted until Christmas Day.

The first victim of this patrol was the Portuguese vessel *Cassequel.* This was a steam freighter that had been built in 1901 and was making for Angola from Lisbon. She was carrying a general cargo and a number of passengers, all of whom survived. The U-108 torpedoed her shortly before 2200 hours.

The other victim of this patrol was part of Convoy HG-76. This was a 1939 built steam freighter that had also left Lisbon but was heading for Oban in Scotland. She was carrying a mixture of food, chemicals and metals. The U-108 torpedoed her at 0615 on the morning of December 19. Two of her forty one crewmembers were killed.

In the New Year, on January 8 1942 the U-108 set sail for its sixth active patrol, returning to Lorient on March 4. This time she was to claim another five victims, all in the February. The first was the brand new British steam freighter *Ocean Venture.* The vessel had left Vancouver and was headed for Hampton Roads, carrying food and aircraft on the deck. The U-108 torpedoed her at 1035 hours on February 8. Thirty one of her forty five crewmembers were killed.

The following day the U-108 torpedoed the Norwegian steam freighter *Tolosa.* She had left Kingston, Jamaica and was making for Chester in Pennsylvania, on the Delaware River. The torpedo attack took place just after 2100 and the twenty two crewmembers were lost.

On February 12 the Norwegian steam freighter *Blink,* carrying phosphates, was torpedoed shortly before 0300 hours. Only six of her thirty crewmen survived this attack. The vessel had left Tampa, Florida and had travelled via Charleston, bound for Halifax and Ipswich.

The next victim fell on February 16 1942. She was the Panamanian steam freighter *Ramapo.* She was torpedoed shortly before 1600 hours. The vessel had left London and was bound for Bermuda and ultimately New York.

The last vessel to be sunk during this patrol was the British steam freighter *Somme,* which had been built in 1919. She had left London and was bound for Bermuda and Curacao, off the Venezuelan coast. The attack took place shortly before 2330 hours on February 18 1942. The crew is presumed to have been lost.

The U-108 set sail for its seventh active patrol on March 30 1942 and again the submarine would claim five victims before returning to Lorient on June 1. The first was the *Modesta,* which was a British steam freighter that had left Trinidad with bauxite onboard and was bound for New York. Seventeen of her crew of forty six were killed when she was torpedoed at around 0830 on April 25.

Four days later, on April 29, the U-108 torpedoed the American steam tanker *Mobil Oil*, which had left New York on April 16 and was bound for Venezuela. The U-108 had been tracking her for some time and in fact it was only after firing six torpedoes at her that the engines were stopped and she began to flood. All fifty two men onboard were saved, but the vessel was finished off by the U-108's deck gun. The victim had not gone down without a fight and had in fact fired at least twelve rounds at the U-108 with its own stern gun. Scholtz had been forced to ceasefire at one point due to defective guns and sights on his own vessel. The loss of this vessel was eventually put down to the captain, who had been told to wait to travel in convoy and had for some reason decided to make the trip alone.

The U-108's next victim was the American steam freighter *Afoundria*, which had left New Orleans, bound for San Juan, in Puerto Rico. The vessel was torpedoed shortly before 2330 hours on May 5 1942.

The penultimate ship claimed by the U-108 in this patrol was the *Abgara*. She was torpedoed at 2211 hours on May 6 1942. She had left Kingston and was bound for Montreal and her crew of thirty four men survived the attack.

The final vessel was the *Norland*, which was bound for Corpus Christi, Texas, having left from the Clyde. She was sunk by a combination of torpedoes and gunfire at around 1840 hours on May 20 1942.

The last active patrol of which Willi Wilke would have taken part was the eighth, which began on July 13 1942 and lasted until September 10. The U-108 claimed three more Allied vessels during this operation. The first was torpedoed at 2220 hours on August 3 1942. This was the 1936 built British motor tanker, *Tricula*. She had left Curacao and Trinidad and was bound for Table Bay in Newfoundland and Labrador. Of the fifty eight men onboard forty seven were killed.

The second vessel was the Norwegian motor freighter *Brenas*, which suffered the same fate as the *Tricula* when it was attacked at 0133 hours on August 7 1942. The captain was taken as a prisoner, one crewmember was killed. The vessel was making for Trinidad and New York when she was hit.

The final vessel that Willi Wilke would have seen go down to the U-108 was the American motor tanker *Louisiana*. She had been built in 1937 and had left Curacao and Trinidad and was bound for Rio de Janeiro. The U-108 torpedoed her shortly before 1700 hours on August 17 1942.

These were undoubtedly the most successful operations for the U-108 and in fact the vessel would only ever go on to claim one more victim. This would be when the vessel was under the command of Ralf-Reimar Wolfram, who commanded the vessel between mid-October 1942 and October 16 1943. The victim was the *Robert Gray*, which was an American steam freighter. She was carrying ammunition out of Baltimore, via New York, to Britain. She had left Baltimore on April 7 and New York on April 12 1943. She fell victim to the U-108 when she was torpedoed at 0313 hours on April 19. Apparently the U-108 had fired a spread of four torpedoes at her from the surface. The *Robert Gray* fired back with her deck gun. The U-108 fired more torpedoes and it is believed that she went down around 0600 hours, after the ammunition onboard set the vessel alight. Thirty nine crewmen and twenty three armed guards were all lost.

The stern torpedo room, as shown in this photograph, was an area of approximately 55sqft. It had eight berths fitted inside it and there was a chain hoist arrangement for handling the torpedoes. These were built into the ship's structure. The Germans used a rather slow method of loading torpedoes from spare stowage. The torpedo was raised from its stowage under the deck and lined up with the tube manually. The Type IXB submarine normally carried twenty two torpedoes. It would have four bow tubes and two stern tubes. The G7eT2 was the standard torpedo, but it suffered from some early teething problems. It was electrically propelled and had a range of 5000m and a speed of 30knots. By mid-1942 an improved version had been introduced, which increased its range by half as much again. This was designated the T3a and could travel at 30knots and had a new range of 7500m.

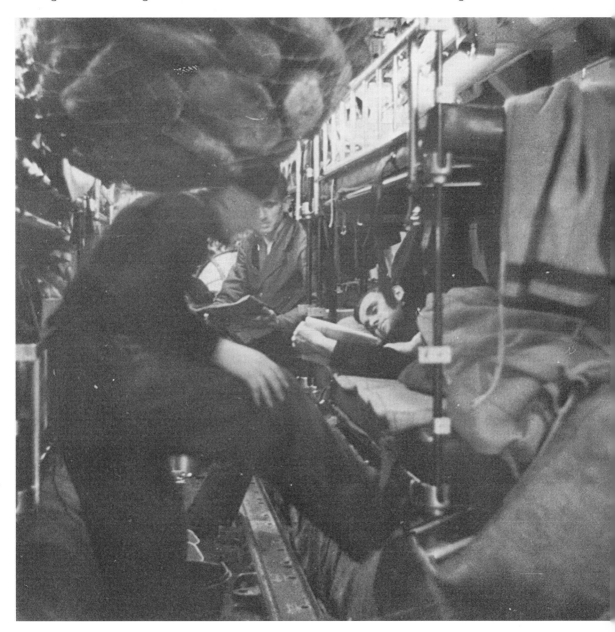

Obermaschinistmaat Werner Todt is in the control room onboard the U-108 in this photograph. It is interesting to note that although this was known as the control room, control of the vessel itself was not centralised. The manoeuvring room and engine room were in one compartment, but they were separated by a watertight bulkhead. If the submarine was using its diesel engines then control would be in the engine room. When it was using its main motors control would be in the manoeuvring room. Just forward of the control room was the main galley of the submarine. It had a small refrigerator, an electric range, sink, hot water heater, soup kettle, a dresser and lockers. The range consisted of three hot plates on top and a hot water heater at the back. Alternatively it would have four hot plates on top and an oven below.

This is another photograph of Werner Todt in the control room of the U-108. The Type IXA and Type IXB submarines both had additional periscopes in the control room, along with the two in the conning tower. From the Type IXC submarines this additional periscope was removed.

This photograph shows an alarm dive in operation in the diesel room of the U-108. At the centre of the photograph is Obermaschinist Stapelmann. The diesel engines had a cylinder diameter of 15.75inches, with a nominal rating of 2170hp and 470rpm. It was a compromised design because in order to get the maximum power for the limited drive rpm it was necessary to supercharge the engine. This was achieved by the exhaust turbine supercharger. Salt water was used to cool the diesel engines, which was considered to be more hazardous than using fresh water. The engines were of a lower speed and quite rugged compared to the Allied submarines.

This photograph is of one of the deck guns, covered in icicles, whilst the U-108 operates in the Baltic Sea during the winter months. Judging by the weather conditions it is probable that this photograph may have been taken during Operation Seerauber, which was a Wolfpack operation that lasted from December 14 1941 to December 23 1942. The U-108 contributed to this Wolfpack operation between December 14 and December 22 1941. Like all Wolfpack operations, this was a joint effort by a number of u-boats. It was during this Wolfpack operation that the U-108 struck the Portuguese vessel *Cassequel* on December 14 and the British vessel *Ruckinge* on December 19.

This photograph shows the crew of the U-108 manning the 105mm anti-ship cannon. This was a semi-automatic weapon and it shared a gun platform with the 88mm gun. It did not have a gun shield and it fired a round weighing 23.3kg. The muzzle velocity was 785m per second and it had a maximum range of 15350m. In many respects the u-boat was not an ideal platform for a gun as big as this. The deck guns lacked range finders and sometimes it was necessary for the crews to be fastened to their positions with life lines. It was only when the u-boat decided to finish off a victim with its deck gun that the weapon really came into its own because the gun and the ammunition would have to be secured and the crew would have to get below deck if the submarine was likely to come under attack. This would all take too long and would put the submarine at risk.

The U-108 is making headway in cold conditions in this shot. Theoretically, the Type IXB could make 18.2knots surfaced and 7.3knots when submerged. Undoubtedly the Type IXB was one of the most successful versions. It had an overall length of 76.5m, a beam of 6.8m, a height of 9.6m and a draft of 4.7m. This version of the u-boat had a theoretical operational range of 24600miles. This meant that they could operate in relatively remote waters. Two prime examples are the U-107 and U-103, which both operated off West Africa. They managed to claim over 330,000tons of Allied shipping between them.

The U-108 is travelling at speed in this photograph, with waves crashing over the bows. The outer shell of the vessel enclosed the bow and stern buoyancy tanks. There were three main ballast tanks, five fuel ballast tanks, a normal fuel oil tank, two variable tanks and a negative tank. The submarine itself was basically a cylindrical pressure hull. It had conical sections at the ends, with cast end bulkheads. The conning tower was oval, with a cast top. The exterior ballast and fuel tanks were inside the envelope of the overall structure. The submergence depth was around 100m.

This photograph shows the U-108 approaching dock. We can clearly see the u-boat emblem in this shot. Initially the emblem was a combination of a shield, cross and crown, but here we can see that the emblem is in fact a polar bear that is standing on ice. It is believed that the original symbol was retained on the conning tower, as we can see a black shield with two crosses. There would have been a matching one on the other side of the conning tower. It is possible that the crosses and the coat of arms is a flotilla symbol. Sometimes these additional emblems were put onto the submarine to denote their home town or port.

A view of the U-108's deck can be seen here, looking towards the conning tower. The submarine has been attached to the side of a large surface vessel and it appears that a resupply is taking place.

This is another view of the U-108, this time from the other side of the conning tower. It does appear from the condition of the deck that the U-108 has just returned from an active service patrol. Note the large vessels in the background. This may suggest that the photograph was actually taken in Wilhelmshaven, rather than in Lorient, which would date this photograph to a period before the middle of March 1941.

The U-108 is making way under a heavy swell in this shot. For much of its active service the U-108 was part of the 2nd Flotilla. Korvettenkapitan Victor Schutze was the commander of the flotilla between August 1941 and January 1943. Schutze had joined the German navy at the age of twenty, in 1925 and he would command the U-25 and the U-103, both of which had active patrols, the latter until the middle of August 1941. He is credited with the sinking of thirty five vessels; seven with the U-25 between October 31 1939 and February 13 1940 and the remainder with the U-103 between October 6 1940 and June 29 1941.

Barely visible in this photograph is the deck gun, in heavy seas. The 2nd Flotilla had been created in early September 1936. Over a period of a year, from June 1940, the flotilla shifted to Lorient. Effectively the flotilla ceased to exist when the last u-boats left Lorient, making for Norway, in August 1944, by which time the bulk of France had been liberated. There was an ever-shifting group of submarines attached to the flotilla and more than ninety served with the 2nd Flotilla between 1936 and 1944. The flotilla was named after a First World War German submarine commander, Reinhold Saltzwedel. He died in December 1917 when his submarine struck a mine in the English Channel.

One member of the crew is emerging into the conning tower in this photograph. Pressure hatches were provided for the upper and lower parts of the conning tower. The diameter of the hatch for the upper conning tower was 555mm. It was fitted with counter springs, latches and dovetailed section gaskets.

One of the crewmen is in his wet weather gear, standing in the conning tower of the U-108, in poor weather conditions. Heavy weather had a negative effect on the submarine's ability to receive communication. There were two receiving antennae; one port and one starboard. They were relatively low and in heavy weather their usefulness would be diminished.

Stormy weather is ahead, as the U-108 ploughs through choppy seas in this photograph. The vessel had a 124 cell battery, with a charging time of around seven hours. The diesel engine would provide power for propulsion or battery charging on the surface.

Inside the control room of the U-108; one of the crew is carefully monitoring the dials and making the necessary adjustments. There were ladders arranged to provide easy access for rapid descent from both the bridge to the control room and from the bridge to the deck guns. There were electric steering stations in the control room and the conning tower. The control room was the main operating station. When the vessel was on the surface there would be five people in the control room, but there would be twice this amount when the submarine was at battle stations.

Keeping a lookout on the U-108; note the manned anti-aircraft gun and the use of the handrail as a position for observation. U-boats depended on visual detection and even in low visibility, at less than two miles; many of them were still spotted by aircraft before the u-boat crews spotted the oncoming attackers. In a large number of cases u-boats failed to dive before being attacked even in good visibility. Data relating to 1941, which combined information that the British had collected on u-boat attacks, showed that when aircraft spotted a u-boat in forty per cent of all cases the submarine had already started to dive. This presumes that the submarine had already seen the aircraft. In another twenty per cent of cases all that was visible to the incoming aircraft was the periscope.

The U-108 is coming alongside a small launch in this photograph. Here we can see the u-boat's emblem, which is visible on the conning tower. Not all u-boats had their own emblems; many of these were training boats. The polar bear emblem is also associated with the 11th Flotilla, which operated out of Norway and was engaged against convoys operating to and from Russia in the Arctic Sea.

Carrying out painting repairs to the emblem and the conning tower are featured here. Each flotilla had its own specific emblem. It is possible to trace the entire history of the nearly 1,200 German U-boats that operated during the Second World War. The German U-boat Museum is in Altenbruch near Cuxhaven.

This is another clear view of the U-108's emblem; the polar bear on ice. It was usual practice for a new captain to add his own emblem, rather than replace the existing emblem on the u-boat. The fear was that if an old emblem was erased then this would bring bad luck to the vessel. The graduating classes would usually choose their own emblem. A prime example is those that graduated in 1936, who inevitably chose the Olympic rings to commemorate the Olympic Games that had been held in Munich that year.

This photograph gives us a good view of the deck gun and manned conning tower of the U-108. Before the war broke out the u-boats would have numerals painted on the conning tower in white, which were about 1.5m tall. These were obviously far too visible in wartime conditions. The u-boats were painted a neutral grey and visible identification was erased, although insignia and emblems were well used across the whole of the submarine fleet.

This is a good close up of the U-108's polar bear standing on ice emblem. Precisely why the U-108 had such an emblem is not known, but they often were representative of some meaning that had a connection to the vessel. Superstition was also a key influence. When Type IIX submarines started to come into service few of these types and later built submarines had emblems, as they rarely surfaced. The tradition of painting emblems and insignia onto the conning tower began to disappear.

Chapter 5

The First Patrol

The U-108, under the command of Scholtz, would carry out eight patrols between October 1940 and October 1942. In all, they would be out to sea on active service for 361 days. The first active patrol out of Wilhelmshaven submarine base was to last for three and a half weeks, during which time the crew sank two vessels.

Wilhelmshaven had been used as a German naval port by the navy for many years. It was both a surface and submarine base and was also an important construction yard. With access into the North Sea and then into the Atlantic it was of great importance to the German war effort. It was heavily defended and the Allies were acutely aware of its importance. The RAF, for example, had launched a disastrous raid in September 1939, which had been a failure and there had been numerous British losses.

The first active patrol was the only patrol launched from Wilhelmshaven during the period in which Willi Wilke served onboard the U-108. After this patrol all of the other active service that he saw focused on the Atlantic.

The first vessel that was to fall to the U-108 had been built in Rotterdam in 1918. She was a steam merchant vessel of just over 1,600tons and her home port was Amsterdam. The *Texelstroom* had left Reykjavik on February 22 1941 and was bound for Grimsby. The vessel went down after being hit by at least two torpedoes just twenty five miles off Iceland and there were no survivors amongst the twenty five crewmembers.

The second vessel that was sunk during this first active patrol was the British merchant ship, the *Effna*, which is looked at in some detail in the next chapter. She was originally built in Seattle in 1919 and transferred to the US reserve fleet before being passed on, in 1940, to the British. Her home port was Newcastle upon Tyne. She was unescorted when the U-108 found her to the southeast of Iceland shortly after 2332 on February 28. The entire crew of thirty three men were killed when she went down, although from the photographs that we will see in the next chapter it appears that all of the crewmembers were alive and well when the U-108 left the scene.

This is a fascinating photograph from the album, which chronicles the operations of the U-108 from the first sailing on February 15 1941 through to the last sailing that involved Wilke, which lasted from July 13 1942 to September 10. It details the number of vessels that were attacked and sunk and their approximate tonnage. However it incorrectly identifies all of the vessels as being British.

Probefahrt E.A.U. T.E.K. U.A.K. und Pillau Juni 1940 – Januar 1941

Fahrt	15. 2. – 12. 3. 1941	2 Dampfer versenkt	12061	BRT
"	3. 4. – 2. 5. 1941	1 Hilfskreuzer "	16644	"
"	25. 5. – 7. 7. 1941	5 Dampfer "	32788	"
"	19. 8. – 21. 10. 1941	– Südatlantik	—	
"	9. 12 – 25. 12 1941	3 Dampfer 1 Tanker "	22360	"
"	8. 1 – 4. 3. 1942	2 Tanker 1 Dampfer	25765	"
"	30. 3. – 1. 6. 1942	2 Tanker 4 "	32255	"
"	13. 7. – 10. 9. 1942	1 " 6 "	36274	"

Bei 3 weiteren Schiffen mit etwa 18000 BRT wurde Sinken nicht beobachtet, da von Zerstörern mehrere Stunden auf 200m gedrückt.

Fahrzeit während des Krieges etwa 25 Monate davon 361 Tage am Fein

This is a photograph of several submarines, including the U-108, in an extremely icy Wilhelmshaven, over the winter of 1940 to 1941. The U-108, having been commissioned towards the end of October 1940, was not fully operational until February 1941. She was assigned to the 2nd u-boat Flotilla that was operating out of Wilhelmshaven and was classed as being under training until her first operational mission. It was a relatively short period of time in which to acclimatise to the requirements of the u-boat and the rigours of active service patrols. The crew had the advantage of Scholtz, who was an experienced man, and although he was well practised on torpedo boats he had little or no knowledge of u-boats until he joined that branch of the service in April 1940. Incredibly he managed to go through significant retraining over a four month period in order to commission the U-108 at the end of October.

The U-108 is alongside the dock at Wilhelmshaven in this photograph. Note that the crew are working on the deck. There is a small, surface vessel alongside the submarine. Scholtz was not the only well known u-boat captain that was linked to the U-108. The last commander of the U-108 was Matthias Brunig, who commanded the vessel between October 1943 and April 1944. Brunig would go on to command the U-3038 between March 4 and May 3 1945.

Crews from other vessels and maintenance men are bidding the U-108 farewell from Wilhelmshaven. When the U-108 left on February 15 1941 the temperature in Wilhelmshaven was 0°C. In the previous few days the temperature had dropped as low as −12°C and in the last few days before the vessel left the temperature had risen, hence the fact that the ice has begun to break up in this photograph.

This photograph shows the U-108 making its way out of Wilhelmshaven. Note the broken sea ice. Wilhelmshaven was a major target for the Allies due to its importance as a major naval base. The U-108 would have shared Wilhelmshaven with the *Sharnhorst* between June and December 1940, as she had been in the port undergoing repairs after an engagement in June 1940. This saw the sinking of the British aircraft carrier, HMS *Glorious*. The *Sharnhorst* had entered the Atlantic through the Denmark Strait on new operations on February 5 1941.

Scholtz is seen in this photograph, alongside the U-108 in Wilhelmshaven shortly before the vessel left the port for its first active patrol. The man on the right of the photograph appears to be an oberleutnant.

Chapter 6

Sinking the Effna

These fifteen photographs are identified in Willi Wilke's album as depicting the last minutes of the British steam merchant vessel, *Effna*. She was carrying steel and trucks from Baltimore via Halifax to Newport. She was attacked by the U-108 somewhere to the southeast of Iceland just after 2330 on February 28 1941. Of particular interest is the fact that the photographs clearly show that the master of the *Effna*, Robert Penney Robertson and his crew were all alive when the *Effna* was sunk. Records also suggest that the *Effna* was in fact sunk by a single torpedo by the U-108. We can clearly see in these photographs, however, that she was in fact sunk by fire from the deck gun.

Unfortunately, although at least seventeen *Effna* crewmen are clearly visible in Wilke's photographs, the life expectancy of these men would have been incredibly low. It was wintertime and to the southeast of Iceland. The men are in an open boat.

The *Effna* had joined Convoy HX-109 at Halifax, Nova Scotia as part of a thirty eight ship convoy that was heading for Liverpool. The convoy had left Halifax on February 13 and during the Atlantic crossing there had been a severe storm. The *Effna* had been amongst several vessels that had fallen behind the convoy. Some ships darted for Iceland and at least one decided to turn back to Halifax.

What is strange is that on February 27 the *Empire Tiger*, another vessel that was part of the convoy, is believed to have picked up an SOS from the *Effna*. It stated her position and said that she was sinking in heavy seas and that the lifeboats had been washed away. It was commonly believed that the *Effna* had been torpedoed by the U-108, but perhaps the submarine had simply finished her off after coming across her in difficulties. The names of all thirty three of the *Effna*'s crewmen are detailed on the Tower Hill memorial.

This is a shot of the *Effna* as a shell from the U-108's deck gun strikes her.

The *Effna* is beginning to keel over. This photograph has been taken relatively close to the vessel. By this stage all of the crew would have been forced to abandon ship.

The *Effna* is going down bow first in this photograph. The crew of the U-108 must have been fairly confident that they would not be observed, as it is clear from this sequence of photographs that they spent a considerable amount of time surfaced around the *Effna* and the lifeboats.

The *Effna* is beginning to disappear beneath the freezing cold waters off Iceland in this shot. None of this sequence of photographs shows any specific damage to the *Effna* and it is still unclear as to why or how she eventually sank.

The *Effna*'s bow is now completely submerged and she has virtually gone down as far as the funnel. Note that there is no smoke or steam plumes rising from the vessel. This must infer that the ship's engines were already either switched off or disabled by the time this photograph was taken. It is also certainly the case that the engines must have been off for some time; otherwise the cold water hitting the hot engines would have caused vapour to appear.

The last seconds of the *Effna* are captured on film here, as only her stern is now visible. This would have been a terrifying sight for the survivors of the crew. They would now know that they were cast adrift and that the submarine would soon leave the vicinity. The chances of survival were incredibly slim.

If we are to believe the captions in Wilke's album then this man is Robert Penney Robertson, who was thirty nine years old and from East Lothian. He was in the merchant navy. It is clear from the photograph that it was taken onboard the submarine and that the u-boat crew were intent on questioning him.

One of the u-boat crewmen is taking careful note of intelligence given by the captain of the *Effna*. The Germans would have been keen to know what the ship was carrying, its route and its intended destination.

The questioning of the captain continues as another member of the submarine crew keeps a careful lookout for prowling Allied aircraft. The *Effna*'s captain would have been keen to know about the submarine's intentions and also be acutely aware of the fact that being left in an open boat so far from shore would mean the men's chances of survival were limited.

This photograph shows what purports to be the surviving crew of the *Effna* on a lifeboat. From the list of the *Effna* crewmembers it is clear that all of the men were members of the merchant navy and that they were all British. However, looking at the individuals in the lifeboat it is clear that some of these men appear to be of Mediterranean origin. This makes the sequence of photographs even more interesting, as this would point to the fact that the photographs were taken considerably later, probably in June 1941 and that they do not show the *Effna* at all, but one of the three Greek vessels that were sunk by the U-108. It could also possibly be the Portuguese vessel that was sunk on December 14 1941.

Three of the crewmen of the *Effna* are precariously balanced on a wooden pallet in this photograph.

This is another photograph of number 4 lifeboat from the *Effna*. It appears to be alongside the U-108 and that this photograph was taken from the conning tower. Clearly visible onboard are fifteen individuals.

The lifeboat is further away from the submarine in this photograph. The survivors would know that they were in a life threatening situation. The chances of being seen either by Allied aircraft or another vessel were low. In any case it was not unknown for u-boats to lurk close to lifeboats in the hope that it would attract another potential victim.

This photograph is captioned as the u-boat crew throwing food to the survivors in the lifeboat. It does appear that the vessel is actually being lowered by the u-boat into the water. This may infer that the lifeboat was picked up by the u-boat and has been used to evacuate the crew of the *Effna*.

The survivors of the *Effna* are making their way from the submarine in this photograph. At the very least the submarine crew would have given them directions to the nearest land and provided food, water and other essentials if possible.

Chapter 7

Lorient

This selection of eight photographs from Willi Wilke's album were all taken in March 1941 and are marked as being just prior to the U-108 leaving Lorient. The U-108 left Lorient on April 3 1941 for its second active patrol. It scored a notable victory on April 13 when it sank the near 16,500ton HMS *Rajputana*. She was a British armed merchant cruiser that had been built in Greenock at the Harland and Wolff shipyard in 1926. The *Rajputana* had actually been completed in December 1925 as a steam passenger ship but the Royal Navy had requisitioned her in December 1939 and had converted her as an armed merchant cruiser. The vessel was to the west of Reykjavik, Iceland on April 13 1941. She was commanded by Captain F H Taylor. The U-108 hit her with a torpedo at around 0745 hours. The U-108 had spotted her on April 11 and had given chase. From the course taken by HMS *Rajputana* it was clear that the crew were perfectly well aware that the u-boat was in the vicinity. The U-108 had great difficulties in keeping track with her due to the ice and snow. She had fired a pair of torpedoes shortly after 1800 hours on April 11, but these had missed. The u-boat tried again just before 2000 hours and these two also missed, as did another pair twenty four hours later.

On April 13 the u-boat had fired a fifth torpedo at 0740 but this also missed and it was not until the sixth shot that she actually hit the vessel in the stern. This caused a fire but did not prevent HMS *Rajputana* from firing back at the u-boat. Yet another torpedo was then fired, at 0823, but this failed to detonate. A final torpedo was fired at 0930 and this time it struck and the vessel began to list and sink stern first.

There were 323 onboard the *Rajputana*; forty men, including the commander of Convoy HX-117, Commander Richardson, were killed. HMS *Legion* managed to pick up the remaining 283 survivors.

The *Rajputana* had been originally operating off the American coast and in the Caribbean between December 1939 and April 1940. In May she transferred to Bermuda and remained there, operating as far as the Canadian coast, until April 1941. When she was sunk on April 13 she had only just joined the North Atlantic Convoy Force.

Members of the crew of the U-108 are parading on the deck of the submarine prior to leaving Lorient. Lorient had been first attacked by the RAF in September 1940. This had prompted the Germans to build extensive bunkers to shelter the u-boats operating from the port. The Germans built a number of shelters, each capable of housing a single u-boat. Construction began in early February 1941, followed by three other similar cathedral-shaped bunkers, the last of which would not become operational until May 1943.

A German band is featured in this photograph, on a merchant vessel. They are playing as the U-108 leaves Lorient. In addition to the three large bunkers six more were built, housing torpedo storage facilities. The bunkers are open to the public. The first Keroman bunker had five pens, the second seven pens and the third had eight pens.

This is another shot of the very overcrowded merchant vessel, with the band and large numbers of German naval personnel seeing the U-108 off for its first mission from the harbour of Lorient. Lorient is located on the south coast of Brittany, providing it with excellent access directly into the Atlantic Ocean. It had been an important fishing port for centuries and in the seventeenth century large warehouses had been built, which were used by the French East India Company. The Germans decided that it was a perfect location for a submarine base. Admiral Donitz gave instructions for the base to be constructed in June 1940 and over the period of the next three years the large concrete u-boat pens were built on the Keroman Peninsular.

Scholtz and members of the U-108 crew are posing for this photograph as they leave Lorient for their first mission in the Atlantic. At its height Lorient was capable of sheltering thirty submarines. The RAF and the USAAF both tried their best to destroy the reinforced concrete submarine pens. The port itself was extensively damaged, but the pens stayed operational. In fact it was still in German hands in May 1945, by which time it had been under siege for some months and the German garrison had refused to surrender.

The U-108 is shown here in Lorient harbour. Of particular interest is the fact that the polar bear on ice emblem has not yet been painted onto the conning tower of the submarine. We must assume that this was done at some point after the first sailing out of Lorient. As the Allies were unable to destroy the submarine pens they tried to destroy the infrastructure around the port of Lorient. Over time it became increasingly more difficult for the Germans to use Lorient as a u-boat base, as they could not get fuel or supplies into the city. In fact by the end of the war around ninety per cent of Lorient had been flattened by aircraft attack. In the short period between mid-January and mid-February 1943, 60,000 incendiaries and 500 bombs were dropped on Lorient.

Part of the crew of the U-108 is parading on the deck on their departure day in this photograph. Note the Kriegsmarine flag flying from the conning tower. At this stage of the war the submarine base was in its infancy, with most of the work being carried out from February 1941 through to 1944. Enormous numbers of foreign workers were brought to Lorient to act as unpaid labourers. The base was the largest of the five German Atlantic coastal bases.

Pennants flutter from the conning tower of the U-108 in March 1941. One of the unsung heroes at Lorient was the Deputy Director of Naval Construction, Jacques Stosskopf. He began working with the Germans in September 1940 and secretly he was sending information to the Allies, telling them of the German submarine movements from the base. He was finally exposed in 1944 and executed but was posthumously awarded the Legion of Honour.

A relaxed captain and crew are on the upper conning tower of the U-108, enjoying their last moments of relaxation before their active patrol in the Atlantic. The other key u-boat bases in this part of France were at Brest, St Nazaire, La Rochelle and Bordeaux. When the Type IX vessels arrived they were for a time the largest that these bases had seen. Later Type XXI vessels would arrive, which were slightly longer than the Type IXB vessels. Brest was home to the 1st and 9th U-boat Flotillas, St Nazaire was the site of the famous raid launched by the British in 1942, La Rochelle was home to the 3rd U-boat Flotilla and Bordeaux was used by both the Germans and the Italians, being an ideal place for the long-range submarines operating in the Atlantic. The Italian submarines were nowhere near as good or successful. In a trial period between October and November 1940 the average German u-boat operating from Bordeaux sank over 1,100tons of enemy shipping per day, against just 20tons sunk by the Italians. Bordeaux would ultimately become the operational base of the 12th Flotilla, with the first u-boat bunker becoming operational in January 1943.

Chapter 8

The Third and Fourth Patrols

It is not clear from the album itself exactly when these photographs were taken. What is apparent is that the U-108 had, for some of the crew, crossed the equator for the first time. This suggests that the U-108 was headed into the South Atlantic. The only clue as to the probable dates of this part of the photograph album is one of the shots that it is dated October 21 1941, which was during the fourth active service patrol of the U-108. The u-boat set off from Lorient on August 19 1941 and returned to base after nine weeks out to sea on October 21 1941. This particular voyage was unsuccessful, although the previous mission that had left Lorient on May 25 1941 and lasted for just over six weeks until July 7 1941 had seen the destruction of seven vessels.

The third voyage of the U-108 had been extremely eventful. The first victim of the U-108 was the British steam merchant ship *Michael E*. At over 7,600tons, she had been built in Glasgow in 1941. She was attacked by the U-108 on June 2 1941. She was part of convoy OB-327 which had dispersed. At around 2043 on June 2, the U-108 had fired two torpedoes at her when she was to the southwest of Cape Clear off the coast of Ireland. One of the two torpedoes hit her in the stern. This nearly crippled the vessel causing her to begin to sink from the stern first shortly after 2220. The torpedo had also killed three of the crew. The remainder of the crew were forced to abandon the vessel (this included the captain, forty-four crew men, two gunners and a dozen RAF men). The survivors of the attack were picked up on June 3 by the Dutch motor merchant ship *Alcinous*.

The *Michael E* was a significant kill for the U-108 as she was the first CAM ship. The CAM ships Catapult Aircraft Merchantman were effectively primitive escort carriers that had a single Hawker Sea Hurricane onboard which was launched by catapult. These vessels did not have the capacity to pick up the aircraft once it had been launched. Therefore, the temporary measure only allowed the safe use of the aircraft provided it was within range of land. The *Michael E* was the first CAM ship that had been converted for the Royal Navy itself (in fact it was the only one for the Royal Navy as all of the others in the series were converted for the Royal Air Force). The *Michael E* had also been the first ship to carry out a test launch off Belfast. At the time, the *Michael E* had left Belfast for normal convoy duties and was bound for Halifax in Canada.

On June 8 1941, the U-108 struck again. This time she attacked the *Baron Nairn* which was part of convoy OB-328. This steam merchant ship had been built in 1925. She was *en route* from Barrow to Nuevitas in Cuba carrying ballast. At around 0006 she was torpedoed by the U-108 to the west of Cape Race, Newfoundland, Canada. Onboard were forty crewmen. When she went down, the crew were split into two groups. The first group of eighteen were picked up by the HMCS *Chambly* and rescued. The other group of twenty men and the captain, John Kerr managed to land on the coast of Galway on June 27. They had been adrift for nineteen days. One of the crew had died although it is not clear whether this was during the attack or in the subsequent series of events. Kerr would later be awarded the Lloyd's War Medal for his bravery.

The U-108 was not content with a single kill on June 8 and also attacked and sunk the Greek vessel *Dirphys*. Although Greek owned with the home port of Chios, she had been built at Sunderland in 1917. She was nearly four and a quarter thousand tons. She had begun life named *Swindon*, she was renamed *Cottesmore*, then in 1920 renamed again to *Avonmede*. In 1925 she had another name change to *Harplion* and was sold into Greek hands in 1931 and christened *Theofano*. She had operated as *Dirphys* since 1937. At shortly after 0600 on June 8 1941, the *Dirphys* was on her own about 600 miles to the east of Newfoundland. She had left Swansea and was bound for Montreal carrying over 6,000 tons of coal. The U-108 torpedoed her and she broke in two and sank very rapidly after her boiler exploded. There were six dead of the twenty five crewmembers onboard and the survivors managed to clamber aboard the single lifeboat that had been launched. Scholtz tried to find out what the vessel had been carrying and where it was headed but gave up and disappeared. The U-108 tried again two days later to extract information from the survivors. This time they took a German speaking crew man from the *Dirphys* onboard the submarine. The man was the Belgian radio operator. After the interrogation, Scholtz gave him the course to the nearest land, some water, bread, two bottles of rum and some matches.

The Norwegian steam merchant ship *Christian Krohg* at just less than two thousand tons was the next victim of the U-108 during this mission. She had been built in 1917 and her homeport was Bergen. She had been part of Convoy OB-329 and was attacked on June 10 1941. She had left London, bound for Oban leaving there on June 1 for St Lawrence carrying ballast. The vessel had already survived a submarine attack back in November 1940 when she had been part of Convoy SC-11. This time she was not to be so lucky. The U-108 had fired a torpedo at her on June 9 and missed, but returned for a second attempt the following day and succeeded in sinking her with the loss of all twenty-three crew men onboard.

At just over three thousand tons, the Greek steam merchant ship *Ellinico* was next on June 25 1941. She had been built in 1904 at Greenock and was now Greek owned operating originally out of Piraeus. Her original name had been *Luchana*, but she had been renamed in 1933 when she passed into Greek ownership. The vessel was part of the dispersed Convoy OG-65. She had left the Mersey on June 14 and was bound for Wabana in Newfoundland. The attack took place at 0620 on June 25 1941 when the U-108 fired a single torpedo at her and she sank by the stern in around three minutes. The U-108 had been stalking her since the previous day having spotted her shortly after 2030 on June 24 and fired two torpedoes at her but missed just before 2400.

The U-108 claimed a second Greek vessel on June 25; this was the *Nicolas Pateras*, of Convoy OB-366. The vessel had been built on the Tyne in 1910 and was originally named *Amsterdam*. Her name then changed to *Brantford* and in 1917 she became *Bayford* then in 1921, after being sold to French owners, she became *Port de la Pallice*. She was sold on to Greek owners in 1924, first becoming *Maria M Diacaki* and ten years later she was renamed *Pente Adelfi* then in 1935 she finally received the name of *Nicolas Pateras*. The vessel was hit by a single torpedo to the south of Greenland at 1614 hours. She had already dispersed from the convoy and it seems that the vessel did not sink and that the U-108 had to surface. This took place about an hour later. The U-108 fired nearly a hundred shots at her before she sank, shortly before 1800 hours.

The final vessel to be sunk on the third active patrol was the British steam merchant vessel *Toronto City*. She had been built in Glasgow in 1925 and named *Nigerian*. She had changed ownership and was renamed in 1935, to become *Kyrenia* and in 1937 another change of ownership saw her renamed the *Toronto City*. The vessel was carrying ballast and heading for St John's in Newfoundland and Labrador. The U-108 spotted her and fired a single torpedo, which hit her in the bow at around 1825 on July 1 1941. The vessel had been operating as a weather observation ship and she went down to the north of the Azores in around three minutes. This was the last act of the third active patrol of the U-108 and she returned to Lorient on July 7 1941.

It is probable that the majority of the photographs that were taken in this part of the album relate to the fourth sailing, which was largely uneventful, but lasted from August 19 to October 21 1941.

Members of the crew are participating in a crossing of the equator ceremony in this shot. Sailors that had already crossed the equator were often referred to as shellbacks, or sons of Neptune. Those that had not crossed the line were nicknamed pollywogs. The pollywogs would have to appear before King Neptune and his court. In many of the ceremonies the crew would dress up as women. The pollywogs would be interrogated by having truth serum administered, in the guise of sauce or aftershave. They would be subjected to embarrassing ordeals.

One of the crew is dressed as King Neptune, with a second crewmember in drag costume. Many aspects of this ceremony had not changed since the eighteenth century. It would begin with King Neptune's procession and the court would be opened, with the pollywog being called for. The individual would be given a medical using oversized instruments and then given medicine made from the foulest ingredients available. The ship's barber would then shave the pollywog. The barber would often be dressed as a butcher, with bloodstains on his white apron.

The shaving ceremony is in progress. Large, wooden razor blades would be used and the barber's foam would often be made of flour and water. The foam would be shaved off whilst the barber held the nose of the pollywog. After this process the pollywog would then be dunked in water and receive a certificate. None of the ship's crew would be immune from this ceremony, regardless of whether or not they were the commanding officer.

Members of the crew are exercising on the deck of the U-108, somewhere near the equator in the late summer of 1941. In the photograph we can clearly see the main deck gun, which was the powerful 105mm gun. Vessels such as the U-108 would have around 110 rounds of ammunition. The Type VI submarine had an 88mm gun, which was not the same as the weapon that was used by the land forces as both a flak gun and an anti-tank gun. Vessels of this type, from around June 1943, would go on patrol in the Atlantic without their deck gun. This weapon was not any use as an anti-aircraft weapon as it could not elevate sufficiently to engage aircraft. By 1943 deck guns were effectively phased out by the Germans, largely as a result of the anti-submarine work by the Allies. It was no longer safe to surface and engage targets with the deck gun.

This is another shot of the equator crossing ceremony, with a number of crewmen suitably dressed. Regardless of the nationality sailors would always follow ancient traditions. It is probable that this ceremony goes back to ancient times, when Neptune, the Roman god of the seas, needed to be appeased. Sacrifices were performed to dissuade Neptune from creating storms.

This photograph shows Heinz-Hugo Lehmann sunbathing in the south Atlantic towards the end of 1941. Lehmann had been born in Dresden in 1915 and had served on the U-32. After his service on the U-108 he went on to serve on the U-1228. This was also a Type IX submarine, which was commissioned in late December 1943. After training out of Hamburg the submarine was attached to the 2nd U-Boat Flotilla, out of Lorient, between August and October 1944. It would then move to Flensburg, where it would remain from November 1944 until the end of the war.

Two unidentified members of the crew are sunbathing near the equator in this photograph. The caption in the photo album positively identifies this photograph as having been taken during the fourth active patrol, between August and October 1941.

A naked motorgerfrieter, Walter Zabel, is carrying out vital maintenance on the deck gun in the south Atlantic, in 1941. The caption in the photo album states that he is cleaning the gun, although presumably it was not necessary to do this with the benefit of a uniform.

Members of the crew of the U-108 are on the deck in this photograph. It is assumed that this photograph was also taken whilst the vessel was in the south Atlantic.

More routine maintenance is being carried out on the deck of the U-108 here, in what must be assumed to be excellent weather conditions. On extended active patrols it was vital that the crew continued to carry out a strict regime of maintenance, cleaning and checking. All ships systems, not just the weaponry, had to be reliable. Once on active patrol the u-boat and its crew was largely alone. There would be limited spares and many of the vessels relied on the expertise and abilities of individuals to improvise.

Chapter 9

Norland

The U-108 sailed out of Lorient on March 3 1942 for its seventh active service patrol. Over the next nine weeks it would sink five vessels including the *Norland*. The four photographs from the album chronicle the dying moments of the Norwegian vessel.

The *Norland* MV was a Norwegian motor tanker that had been built in 1941 by the Blythswood Shipbuilding Company at Yard No.64 in Scotstoun, Glasgow. The vessel was originally called the *Empire Pict*, and she was a diesel powered vessel. Under her new name, she made her first sailing leaving the Clyde on May 20 1942. She was part of Convoy ON-93 and left the convoy as planned and was torpedoed by the U-108.

The *Norland* did not sink immediately, her engines were still working and she tried to get away. The U-108 fired again and the Germans ordered her crew to abandon ship. The *Norland's* crew complied and got aboard lifeboats. The U-108 deployed its deck gun to finish off the *Norland*, having to fire several times at her before she succumbed to the punishment and slipped beneath the waves. One of the lifeboats was picked up by the Dutch vessel *Polyphemus*, which was also sunk by a German submarine. Incredibly, although many of the *Polyphemus*' crew perished, all of the crew of the *Norland* subsequently survived.

The *Norland* had arrived in the UK as part of Convoy HX-182. She would leave Glasgow bound for Corpus Christi, Texas with Convoy ON-93. The convoy itself had left Liverpool and the *Norland*, according to plan had left the convoy on May 8 1942.

As far as the maritime enquiry is concerned over the sinking of the *Norland* she was hit by a torpedo fired by the U-108 at around 1257 (German logged time 1839). At the time she was proceeding at around 12.5 knots in fairly clear weather in a moderate sea. The wind was Force 3 and southeast. There was excellent visibility as can be seen in the four photographs which chronicle her loss. No other ships were in sight when she was attacked.

The *Norland* presumably after it had been already hit by a torpedo fired by the U-108. When the attack from the U-108 came, there were four lookouts (the Second Mate, the Helmsman and another on the bridge and the fourth man on the top of the wheelhouse). The aft gun was already manned by three crewmen. It is reported that the U-108's torpedo hit the *Norland* with some force in No.8 tank which was forward of the bridge on the starboard side of the vessel. The torpedo hit around 10 feet below the waterline and tore a hole in her of around 50-60 feet. Initially, the captain had been in his quarters when the attack happened, the Second Mate (presumably) ordered that the lifeboats be launched and for the crew to abandon ship. When the captain arrived on the bridge it was apparent that despite the damage the *Norland* was not actually sinking. He countermanded the order. Also the engines had been stopped, but again the captain ordered them to be restarted and for the vessel to proceed at full speed away from the danger. The captain also ordered the vessel to make for Bermuda and ordered the turn accordingly.

The *Norland* at closer quarters after having been hit by the deck gun of the U-108, the submarine is moving in for the final kill. There was no further contact or action by the U-108 for the next ten minutes or so. However, one of the *Norland*'s crew spotted a periscope some 6 miles off. The captain ordered the ship's 4" gun to fire on the target. The U-108 promptly disappeared, but she had not given up. She surfaced around half an hour later and began to shell the *Norland* with her main deck gun. The *Norland* still refused to give up and replied with around 20 shots of her own. The *Norland* was, however, crippled and she could not get away from the U-108. Slowly but surely, the shots from the U-108 were getting more accurate and the captain reluctantly ordered the ship's engines to be stopped, he ordered that an SOS be transmitted detailing the *Norland*'s position and the fact she was under fire from a German submarine. The captain finally gave orders for the ship to be abandoned at around 1500. Three lifeboats were launched. The 1st Mate and 18 other crew were in the first boat, the captain and 14 others in the second and the 2nd Mate and 13 others in the third. As the lifeboats pulled away, they remained close to the *Norland* who had by this stage caught fire. She was blazing amidships and aft. By this time, she was also visibly sinking. The crew would later suggest that at least 200 shots had been fired at the *Norland* by the submarine's deck guns. With no other option, the three boats set a course for Bermuda and moved away from the stricken vessel.

A photograph showing the last minutes of the *Norland* before she finally succumbs to the damage inflicted on her by the U-108. The three lifeboats managed to keep close to one another for three to four days. Poor weather would mean that they would lose sight of one another. There was heavy rain on the afternoon of May 23 and one boat disappeared from view. The second boat was lost to view from the captain's boat on the afternoon of May 25. Incredibly, all forty-eight of the men would be picked up and rescued. The US Coast Guard cutter 453 found the captain's boat shortly before 1600 on June 7 off Cape Lockout and took them into Morehead City, North Carolina. The lifeboat with the fourteen men aboard had been picked up by the Dutch vessel *Polyphemus* close to Bermuda on May 25. Their ordeal was not yet over. The U578 torpedoed her on May 26 and once again they had to clamber into lifeboats along with the crew of the *Polyphemus*. The fourteen men of the *Norland* managed to survive both torpedo attacks.

A photograph showing the *Norland* as she keels over and begins to sink. From the slight blurring in the photograph, it is clear that she is keeling over at a fast rate and is on the verge of submerging forever. The *Polyphemus* was carrying wheat and wool from Australia. She had left Sydney on April 16 and had reached Balboa on May 10. Her ultimate destination was Great Britain. She had stopped over in Cristobal for engine repairs and had left for Halifax on May 16. She was forced to turn back due to engine problems and had had additional repairs before setting off again on May 19. She had picked up the fourteen men of the *Norland* on May 25. The *Polyphemus* was around 350 miles to the north of Bermuda on May 26 when she was torpedoed shortly after 1800. The U578 hit her with two torpedoes on her starboard side. Some fifteen of her Chinese crew were killed as they were resting in their quarters. The vessel was crippled in the attack and the captain (Koningstein) ordered the lifeboats to be launched and the ship was abandoned. Five lifeboats were launched. The U578 surfaced to question the crew, handed over a carton of cigarettes and disappeared. The crew then watched as the *Polyphemus* sank by the stern at around 1700. Three of the lifeboats were found near Nantucket and the other two were saved by the crew of a Portuguese vessel (*Maria Amelia*). Bizarrely, before this had happened another German submarine had surfaced near one of the lifeboats and had demanded to know the name of the ship and how and where it had been sunk. The submarine's crew wished them well and then disappeared. The Portuguese vessel was more fortunate than the other two and managed to get to New York where the survivors were put ashore and later made their way back to Great Britain.

Bibliography and Websites

www.uboat.net
www.uboataces.com
www.kriegsmarine-reich.co.uk
www.feldgrau.com
www.ubootwaffe.net

Buchheim, Lothar-Gunther, *U-boat War*, Alfred A Knopf, 1978
Canwell, Diane and Jon Sutherland, *U-Boats in World Wars One & Two*, Maritime History Books, 2009
Edwards, Bernard, *War of the U-boats*, Maritime History Books, 2007
Macintyre, Donald, *The Battle of the Atlantic*, Pen & Sword, 2006
Mars, Alastair, *Unbroken*, Pen & Sword, 2008
Paterson, Lawrence, *U-Boats Combat Mission, The Pursuers & the Pursued: First-hand Accounts of U-Boat Life and Operations*, Chatham Publishing, 2007
Paterson, Lawrence, *U-Boats in the Mediterranean 1941-1944*, Chatham Publishing, 2007
Vause, Jordan, *U-boat Ace*, Naval Institute Press, 2003
Werner, Herbert, *Iron Coffins*, Cassell, 1999
Williams, Andrew, *The Battle of the Atlantic*, BBC Books, 2003
Williamson, Gordon, *Wolfpack*, Osprey 2006